Let's Sit Down and
MEDITATE

WRITTEN BY KATIE STOECKELER

ILLUSTRATED BY SARA MARTIN

ISBN: 9798605347125

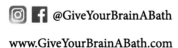 @GiveYourBrainABath

www.GiveYourBrainABath.com

For my Dad
I miss you every day.

Have you ever felt so tired you could fall right to sleep?

Even with five hundred snakes
slithering at your feet?

Have you ever found it hard to focus, or didn't notice someone calling your name?

How about while doing homework, reading, or playing a video game?

Well, let me teach you a
SUPERPOWER
that we all possess within.

You always have it when you're angry,
sad, or find it hard to grin.

It's called MEDITATION
and it's wonderful, you'll see.

In no time at all,
PEACE will come to be.

Just as we shower, brush our teeth,
and practice reading and math,
we meditate to cleanse our thoughts
and give our brains a bath.

Don't overthink it,
it's easy to do.
Meditation
will bring out the

BEST

side of you!

To begin, sit cross-legged or
on your heels with bent knees.
If you find your mind wanders,
just remember to

BREATHE.

Get comfy,
wrap yourself in a blanket or two.
Maybe your favorite friend
wants to join you!

Maybe you'd like to sit on a
special mat or pillow.
Let your arms hang loosely
like a lovely weeping willow.

Sit in

SILENCE and

STILLNESS,

trust you'll

feel **FREE** and

LIGHT soon.

Like a beautiful
butterfly
emerges from
its cocoon.

It's natural...

...for thoughts...

...to FLOAT by.

You can watch
them drift,
but don't
welcome them
or say "hi."

Focus on your **BREATH**
as you fill your belly with air.

Meditation is one of
the best ways to practice

SELF-CARE.

It's normal in the beginning
to want to move
or feel sore.

Start off by meditating for
ONE MINUTE
and you'll find you
begin to crave more.

Afterwards you'll feel a

CALMNESS

within, but while you
meditate,
don't focus on an itch
on your skin.

The itch
will eventually dissipate,
like challenges in life
that arise.

ITCH

Meditation allows us
to connect to ourselves;
it reminds us that we are

CAPABLE AND WISE.

27

You see, meditation carries
into everyday life.
It teaches us how to

RESPOND

rather than react,
preventing lots of frustration
and strife.

When we react, we give power to things that make us feel bad, leaving us

angry

disappointed

and sad.

When we respond, we come from a more grounded place of

LOVE.

We don't have regrets or thoughts of "should of."

You're doing something new that's out of your comfort zone.

Just remember,
meditation is like welcoming yourself HOME.

If you ever feel worried, upset, or unsure of what to do...

...remember the

STRENGTH

you have within you.

Release all your
worries,
do not wait!
It's time
to sit down and

MEDITATE!

TIPS FOR PARENTS & TEACHERS

To Discuss BEFORE Meditation

Let's try to sit in each position and see which one feels more comfortable to us—cross-legged or on your heels with bent knees.

Take a moment to see which feels more comfortable: pick something to gaze at or close your eyes all together. If you choose to gaze at something, be sure to choose a spot that isn't distracting (like a spot on the wall).

If you find your mind wandering as you meditate, remember to concentrate on your breathing. It may be helpful to put your hands on your belly and feel it expand like a balloon as you inhale… let's practice together.

A reminder before we mediate: sometimes bad thoughts may creep into our mind as they may do throughout our day or when we are sleeping at night. This is normal…just concentrate on your breath and let any bad thoughts continue floating by.

TIPS FOR PARENTS & TEACHERS

To Discuss AFTER Meditation

Why do we meditate?
To give our brains a bath, to calm our bodies and minds, to relieve stress, to feel better.

How do we meditate?
We sit cross-legged or on bent knees; we rest our gaze or close our eyes;
we sit in silence and stillness; if our mind wanders we take deep breaths.

Why is meditation important?
It helps us let go of worries and stress; it helps us focus; it helps us to feel calm and happy; it helps us relax.

What was your favorite part of the book and why?

How does the book make you feel?

Can you relate to any characters in the book? Why or why not?

Can you think of a time in your life when you were sad or mad or upset that mediation could have helped you?

For free enrichment resources, visit www.GiveYourBrainABath.com

SCAVENGER HUNT

1   The more we meditate, the more we feel calm and bright.
    Look for two hearts on one page—one dark and one light.

2   Peace is all around us; it's everywhere we look.
    How many peace signs can you find in and on this book?

3   All living things feel love, all animals—event ants!
    Can you find a happy, meditating plant?

4   It doesn't matter if you live in an apartment, house or igloo—
    Anyone can meditate, including me and you.
    You'll see that friends of all colors, ages, and sizes can meditate, too.
    Finding the page with different types of homes is the challenge I have for you.

5   Humans and animals have different things that stress them; I'm sure you can relate.
    Can you find the page that shows that even fish meditate?

6   While it is important to challenge yourself and always try your best,
    An owl shows us on this page that everyone needs rest.

7   You're getting awfully good at this, I never would have guessed!
    But can you find the page that has a picture of a test?

8   There's a girl on this page who is so overwhelmed;
    she doesn't even notice the yummy dinner plate.
    Can you find her? And, more importantly, can you relate?

9   You probably have an agenda for school that reminds you of reading, writing and math.
    Can you locate the rubber ducks that remind you to give your brain a bath?

10 The author and the illustrator worked hard to make this book fun for you!
    Where can you find information about them and learn more about what they do?

11 The time has come to say goodbye and bid you all adieu.
    Can you guess which illustration shows the author who wrote this scavenger hunt for you?

Answers:

1. See the butterfly wings on page 21.
2. See the four peace signs, found on the cover, and pages 11, 34, 36.
3. See page 17.
4. See pages 32-33.
5. See page 14.
6. See the cuckoo clock on page 24.
7. See page 29.
8. See pages 8-9.
9. See the cover, title page, and page 12.
10. See the back cover.
11. See pages 11 and 36.

GLOSSARY

comfort zone: a place or experience that feels comfortable

crave: to want

dissipate: to go away

emerge: to come out of

frustration: feeling angry or upset because you cannot do or change something

meditation: to train attention and awareness, and achieve a calmer or more relaxed state by focusing on your breathing

possess: to have or to own

respond: to reply (in action or words)

strife: a conflict or something that is difficult

Made in the USA
Middletown, DE
11 September 2022

73433870R00022